fruit

fruit

SUZIE SMITH

PERIPLUS

All about fruit 6

Savory dishes 10

Chicken stuffed with prunes • Roast chicken with pickled kumquats and polenta • Beef fillet braised with quinces • Osso bucco with oranges and lemons • Lamb cutlets with red currants and cherries • Moroccan lamb tagine with apricots • Escallops of pork with purple grapes • Spicy citrus-pickled shrimp • Salmon fillets with mango salad and basil oil

Salads and side dishes 28

Green papaya and butternut squash salad • Kiwifruit, cucumber, orange and cashew salad • Mango and red bell pepper salsa • Tropical fruit salad with lime syrup

Cakes, pies, and pastries 32

Apple and date cake • Apple pie • Blueberry cheesecakes • Blueberry and almond mini muffins • Kiwifruit sponge cake • Lemon tart • Old-fashioned lemon cake • Orange cake with plum glaze • Chocolate pear tartlets • Upside-down pear gingerbread • Warm banana cake with caramel bananas • Strawberry shortcakes

Poached fruit 52

Pears in black currant syrup • Peaches with vanilla custard • Plums with Bavarian cream

Sauces for sweets 58

Blackberry sauce • Mango and passion fruit sauce • Gingered litchi sauce

Desserts 62

Bread-and-butter berry puddings • Dark cherry trifle • Baked apples • Panfried pineapple • Brandied pear, cherry and apricot crumble • Strawberries and mangoes with zabaglione • Strawberries in raspberry cream • Watermelon gelatin • Whiskey oranges

Sorbets and ices 78

Cantaloupe sorbet • Raspberry and ricotta semifreddo • Watermelon and lime granita
• Pink grapefruit granita

Dried fruit 84

Rich chocolate and dried fruit cake • Dried fruit and lemon tea compote • Dried-apricot jam

Jams and jellies 88

Raspberry jelly • Strawberry jam • Quince jam • Orange and lime marmalade

Preserves, relishes, and chutneys 94

Mango chutney • Fresh pineapple pickle • Preserved lemons
• Spiced cherries

Marinades 98

Cranberry marinade • Raspberry marinade • Thai lime marinade
• Red wine, cherry and thyme marinade • Sweet-and-spicy sour pineapple marinade
• Grapefruit and honey marinade

Drinks 104

Pineapple-lime cooler • Healthy yogurt-fruit drink • Iced lemon tea
• Low-fat banana smoothie • Lemon-limeade

Index 108
Guide to weights and measures 111

f r u i t

ALL ABOUT
fruit

f or many of us, life would not be the same without our daily fruit. Fruit is nature's special vitamin pill. It is also nature's way of adding a little healthy sweetness to our diets. Whether we enjoy slices of refreshing mango in summer or a wedge of hot apple pie in winter, fruit is a succulent, healthy indulgence the year around.

The recipes in *Fruit*, from salads and main courses to desserts, drinks and preserves, emphasize the use of fruit at its seasonal peak — the best way to guarantee quality. When fruit is allowed to ripen on the vine or on the tree before it is harvested and sent to market, its natural sugars are able to develop their appealing sweetness, its flesh reaches ideal taste and texture, and its fragrance becomes intense and alluring. For this reason, it is important to note when fruits are in and out of season. Although modern methods of transportation and refrigeration have increased the seasonal and geographic availability of many fruits, some varieties that are picked when too immature or are grown in hothouses and shipped long distances — or are stored too long before arriving at the market — have inferior taste and texture. Local growers who bring the products of their harvest to farmers' markets are one of our prime sources of ripe, flavorful fruits at their seasonal best.

Spring and summer are the seasons of great abundance and wide selection. The flesh of these fruits is soft, sweet and juicy, the colors bright and warm, the aromas intense and full. Pineapples, papayas, coconuts, passion fruit and other topical varieties begin to appear in the spring. With the approach of summer, strawberries, blackberries, blueberries, red and black currants and a vast array of stone fruits — peaches, nectarines, apricots, plums and cherries —

reach the market, ready to quench us during the heat of a summer day. Summer is also the time for us to appreciate figs and mangoes, two of the most deliciously succulent and desirable of all fruits.

As summer leads to autumn, apples, pears, quinces and kiwifruit (Chinese gooseberries) come into season. The skin and flesh of fall's fruits are not as bright and blushed as summer's varieties, and the textures are crisper — a characteristic that these fruits have evolved to protect their seeds from the harsh elements of winter. Fruits of autumn reach their peak in winter, when we long for warm poached fruit accompanied with custard or fruits baked until soft and sweet in tarts and pies. Oranges and grapefruits are also at their peak in winter, providing us with vitamins that ward off winter colds and flus. Once again, nature responds to the needs of our bodies and our temperaments.

A question you may ponder when faced with all these choices in the market is, Why are some fruits, such as tomatoes and eggplants (aubergines), considered vegetables? The distinction is largely based on taste and custom. For culinary purposes, we have reclassified these two members of the nightshade family and other fruits — like corn, shelling beans and olives — as vegetables because they are not as sweet as most other fruits and have flavors and textures better suited for use in savory recipes.

From the botanical point of view, peaches, apples, berries and all other fruits, including tomatoes and eggplants, are the mature products of flowering plants — whether bushes, trees or vines — and are the structures that bear the seeds of those plants. After the flowers of a plant are pollinated, the flesh of the fruit grows around the

fertilized seed to protect it as it develops. If the mature fruit is not harvested, it drops from the plant, the flesh falls away, and the seeds can germinate. Not all fruits are fleshy. Some, like shelling beans, are dry. When the pod matures on the plant, it splits open and releases its seeds. Vegetables, in contrast, may be the roots, stems, leaves, buds, flowers, pods or seeds of the plant.

As varied and versatile as vegetables are, it is hard for us to imagine serving baked eggplant or a dish of olives for dessert. Fruits, though, are delicious in both sweet and savory dishes and are welcome additions to every course of a meal, from salads and main courses to desserts and beverages. Once associated chiefly with dessert, fruits are among the most versatile fresh ingredients in the kitchen.

A plump, ripe fig or a slim wedge of juicy cantaloupe (rock melon) swathed in a paper-thin piece of prosciutto is a creation unto itself. The sweetness of the fruit contrasts perfectly with the saltiness and fine bite of the cured ham. This balance of taste and texture explains why fruits so effectively enhance savory dishes, as they do in the recipes in this book. Slices of fresh lemon and lime impart their characteristic tartness and acidity to marinated shrimp (prawns), and apricots add their sweetness to lamb permeated with Moroccan spices. In other recipes, purple grapes are paired with pork, cherries and red currants with lamb, and mangoes with salmon, and fruit marinades are used to flavor and moisten barbecued foods. In all these savory dishes, fruit adds complexity and interest to meats, poultry, seafood and vegetables.

As valuable a place that fruit has in the world of savory dishes, it is an utter pleasure enjoyed in pies, cakes, sorbets and other desserts. The intriguing combinations seem boundless: oranges laced with whiskey and garnished with toffee, strawberries dressed with raspberry cream, poached peaches surrounded by vanilla custard and ice cream topped with warm mango and passion fruit sauce. Classic desserts like apple pie, lemon cake and fruit sorbets never fail to satisfy us. Fruit in season, already beautiful and delicious on its own, can be transformed into an infinite array of desserts both spectacular and sublime.

Preserved in one season to be enjoyed in the next, dried fruits find their own special place in savory dishes and desserts such as rich, dark cakes and compotes. When pears, figs, apricots and other fruits are dried, their sugar content is concentrated as their moisture is removed, intensifying their sweetness and giving their flesh a delectable chewiness. A little dried fruit goes a long way — each small piece has big flavor.

With each piece of fruit, there is often a tale to be told or a recipe to be savored or anticipated. Perhaps you remember the victorious battle with the blackberry bush to harvest its berries or the juicy bite of a new-season peach discovered at a farmers' market. Maybe the first quinces of autumn inspire you to make jam for the winter or the availability of your favorite apple variety prompts you to make a pie to savor some chilly evening by a warm fire. The recipes in *Fruit* will encourage you to appreciate nature's bounty throughout the seasons.

Chicken stuffed with prunes

8 boneless, skinless chicken breast halves (about
4 oz/250 g each)

24–32 pitted prunes

1 tablespoon vegetable oil

3 cloves garlic, crushed

¹/₄ cup (2 fl oz/60 ml) olive oil

¹/₂ cup (4 fl oz/125 ml) red wine vinegar

¹/₂ cup (4 fl oz/125 ml) white wine

¹/₃ cup (2¹/₂ oz/75 g) packed brown sugar

3 bay leaves

¹/₂ cup (¹/₂ oz/15 g) fresh oregano leaves

2 tablespoons drained capers

¹/₂ cup (6 oz/180 g) green olives

Preheat oven to 350°F (180°C/Gas 4).
Make incision in thickest part of
each chicken breast half and stuff
with three or four prunes. Heat vegetable
oil in large frying pan over medium-high
heat. Cook chicken until browned on
both sides, about 2 minutes. Place in
ovenproof baking dish large enough to
accommodate chicken in one layer.
Combine remaining ingredients and pour
over chicken. Bake until chicken is tender
and golden, about 40 minutes.

To serve, place one breast half on each
plate. Pour sauce over chicken.
Accompany with rice or buttered baby
potatoes, or with a simple green salad.

Serves 8

Roast chicken with pickled kumquats and polenta

FOR PICKLED KUMQUATS

1 lb (500 g) kumquats

1 teaspoon salt

4 cups (32 fl oz/1 L) boiling water

$^3/_4$ cup (5 oz/150 g) superfine (caster) sugar

8 cardamom pods, gently crushed

1 cinnamon stick

2 cups (16 fl oz/500 ml) white or red wine vinegar

FOR CHICKEN AND POLENTA

4 chicken breast halves with wings and skin
   attached (about 300 g/10 oz each)

1 tablespoon olive oil

salt and freshly ground pepper

6 cups (48 fl oz/1$^1/_2$ L) water

1$^1/_2$ cups (7$^1/_2$ oz/235 g) polenta

1$^1/_2$ cups (12 fl oz/375 ml) chicken stock

10 oz (300 g) baby spinach leaves

To make pickled kumquats, place kumquats in large glass or ceramic bowl. Dissolve salt in boiling water and pour over kumquats. Let stand, covered, at room temperature for 12 hours. Drain. Combine remaining ingredients in large saucepan over low heat, stirring to dissolve sugar. Raise heat, bring vinegar mixture to boil and cook until slightly syrupy, about 5 minutes.

Pack kumquats in 4-cup (32-fl oz/1-L) sterilized jar and pour in vinegar mixture. If mixture does not reach top of jar, fill with boiling water. Seal jar immediately. Store in cool place for at least 1 week before using. Kumquats will keep for at least 6 months on shelf or for 1 month in refrigerator after opening.

To make chicken and polenta, preheat oven to 350°F (180°C/Gas 4). Place chicken breast halves on rack in roasting pan. Brush with olive oil and season with salt and pepper. Bake chicken, basting two or three times with pan juices, until meat is tender and juices run clear when pricked with skewer between wing and breast, about 25 minutes.

Meanwhile, place water in large saucepan, salt lightly and bring to boil. Stir in polenta and cook over low heat, stirring constantly, until polenta is smooth and no longer grainy, about 20 minutes.

Remove chicken from oven, place on platter, cover and set aside in warm place. Skim as much fat as possible from pan and place over medium heat. Strain 1/4 cup (2 fl oz/60 ml) pickling liquid from jar of kumquats into pan and bring mixture to boil. Cook 1 minute. Transfer to small saucepan and add chicken stock. Return mixture to boil and cook until slightly thickened, about 5 minutes. Add kumquats and simmer over low heat until kumquats are slightly softened, about 0 minutes. Season sauce with salt and pepper.

To serve, place polenta in middle of each plate and top with spinach and chicken breast. Pour sauce and kumquats over top.

Serves 4

ROAST CHICKEN WITH PICKLED KUMQUATS AND POLENTA

Beef fillet braised with quinces

2 tablespoons olive oil

2 lb (1 kg) beef fillet

salt and freshly ground pepper

2 onions, cut into eighths

1 cup (8 fl oz/250 ml) dry white wine

1 cup (8 fl oz/250 ml) beef stock

$^1/_2$ cup (4 fl oz/125 ml) grape juice

2 quinces, peeled, cored and cut into eighths

3 sprigs thyme

$^1/_2$ cup (3 oz/90 g) raisins (optional)

Heat 1 tablespoon oil in ovenproof pan large enough to accommodate beef. Cook beef briefly over medium-high heat until browned on all sides. Season with salt and pepper. Drain beef on plate lined with paper towels.

Heat remaining 1 tablespoon oil in same pan and add onions. Cook over medium heat, stirring, until soft, about 5 minutes. Combine wine, stock, and grape juice, add to pan and bring to boil. Add quince pieces, thyme and raisins if desired and simmer, uncovered, until quinces just begin to soften, about 20 minutes.

Preheat oven to 350°F (180°C/Gas 4). Return beef to pan and spoon quince mixture over meat so it is well covered. Cover with tight-fitting lid and bake until beef is tender and quinces are soft, about 30 minutes. Transfer beef, quinces and onions to serving platter. Bring remaining juices to boil. Boil rapidly until sauce reduces by one-third, 5–7 minutes.

To serve, slice beef and arrange on plates with quinces and onions. Spoon sauce over top. Accompany with roasted potatoes.

Serves 4

BEEF FILLET BRAISED WITH QUINCES

Osso bucco with oranges and lemons

FOR OSSO BUCCO

3 tablespoons olive oil

1 onion, sliced

2 carrots, peeled and sliced

2 small celery sticks, sliced

2 cloves garlic, crushed

2 pieces lemon peel (2 in/5 cm long), cut into
thin strips

2 pieces orange peel (2 in/5 cm long), cut into
thin strips

2 tablespoons all-purpose (plain) flour

8 pieces veal or beef shank (about 1 in/2^1/$_2$ cm thick)

2 bay leaves

1 cup (8 fl oz/250 ml) dry white wine

2 cups (16 fl oz/500 ml) beef stock

2 cups (13 oz/400 g) chopped tomatoes

3 potatoes (about 10 oz/300 g), peeled and quartered

FOR GREMOLATA

3 tablespoons chopped fresh parsley

1 tablespoon finely grated lemon zest

2 cloves garlic, finely chopped

Heat 1 tablespoon olive oil in large ovenproof pan over medium-low heat. Add onion, carrots, celery and garlic. Cook, uncovered, stirring, until onions are soft, 5–7 minutes. Remove pan from heat and stir in lemon and orange peel. Place flour on large plate and dust each shank piece with flour. Heat remaining 2 tablespoons olive oil in large frying pan over medium-high heat. Cook shank pieces until browned on both sides, about 2 minutes. Season with salt and pepper. Drain on plate lined with paper towels.

Preheat oven to 300°F (150°C/Gas 2).

Add shank pieces to onion mixture. Return pan to medium-high heat, add bay leaves, wine, stock and tomatoes and bring to boil. Add potatoes, cover with tight-fitting lid, reduce heat to low and cook until meat is tender and sauce is thick, about 1^1/2 hours.

To make gremolata, combine all ingredients in small bowl.

To serve, place osso bucco, vegetables, and sauce on plates. Sprinkle generously with gremolata. Accompany with noodles or rice.

Serves 4

Lamb cutlets with red currants and cherries

1 tablespoon olive oil

8 lamb cutlets (about 1 1/2 lb/750 g), trimmed

1/4 cup (2 fl oz/60 ml) orange juice

1/2 cup (4 fl oz/125 ml) chicken stock

2 tablespoons red wine vinegar

2 tablespoons packed brown sugar

1 cinnamon stick

1 cup (8 oz/250 g) pitted, sweet dark cherries

3/4 cup (4 oz/125 g) red currants

salt and freshly ground pepper

Heat oil in large frying pan over medium-high heat. Cook cutlets until browned on both sides, about 8 minutes. Set cutlets aside, covered, in warm place.

Add orange juice, stock and vinegar to pan and bring to boil. Boil 3–4 minutes. Add remaining ingredients and simmer until sauce is heated through and cherries and red currants are slightly soft, 3–4 minutes. Season to taste with salt and pepper.

Serve cutlets with mashed potatoes and top with sauce.

Serves 4

LAMB CUTLETS WITH RED CURRANTS AND CHERRIES

Moroccan lamb tagine with apricots

FOR LAMB

2 tablespoons all-purpose (plain) flour

salt and freshly ground pepper

1^1/$_2$ lb (750 g) lamb from leg or shoulder, cut into 1-in (2^1/$_2$-cm) cubes

3 tablespoons olive oil

1 onion, sliced

1 teaspoon ground coriander

1 teaspoon ground cumin

^{1}/$_2$ teaspoon ground cardamom

^{1}/$_2$ teaspoon cardamom seeds

2 cloves garlic, crushed

3 cups (24 fl oz/750 ml) chicken stock

^{3}/$_4$ cup (4 oz/125 g) dried apricots

^{1}/$_2$ lemon, thinly sliced

8 fresh apricots, halved and pitted

^{1}/$_4$ cup (^{1}/$_3$ oz/10 g) chopped fresh parsley, for garnish

FOR COUSCOUS

2 cups (12 oz/315 g) instant couscous

salt

2 cups (16 fl oz/500 ml) boiling water

3 tablespoons butter (optional)

To make lamb, place flour and salt and pepper to taste in plastic bag. Add lamb pieces and shake until pieces are coated. Heat 2 tablespoons oil in large heavy saucepan over medium-high heat. Add lamb pieces, in batches, and cook, stirring, until browned on all sides, 3–4 minutes. Drain lamb on plate lined with paper towels.

Heat remaining 1 tablespoon oil in pan over medium heat and add onion. Cook until soft, about 5 minutes. Add spices and garlic and cook 1 minute. Return meat to pan and add stock and dried apricots. Bring to boil and simmer, uncovered, stirring occasionally, for 1 hour.

Add lemon slices and fresh apricots and simmer until apricots are tender about 10 minutes. Season to taste with salt and ground pepper.

To make couscous, place couscous in large bowl. Lightly salt boiling water and pour over couscous. Cover immediately and let stand, uncovered, for 10 minutes. Remove cover and fluff grains with fork. Stir in butter if desired.

Serve lamb with couscous. Sprinkle with parsley.

Serves 4

MOROCCAN LAMB TAGINE WITH APRICOTS

Escallops of pork with purple grapes

8 slices brioche (about $^1/_2$ in/1 cm thick)

$^1/_4$ cup (2 fl oz/60 ml) olive oil

2 oz (60 g) butter

8 pieces boneless pork (about 1 lb/500 g),
  flattened with mallet

salt and freshly ground pepper

$^1/_4$ cup (2 fl oz/60 ml) dry white wine

$^1/_2$ cup (4 fl oz/125 ml) chicken stock

$1^1/_2$ cups (12 oz/375 g) seedless purple grapes

Preheat oven to 350°F (180°C/Gas 4). Brush brioche slices with oil and place in single layer on baking sheet. Bake until golden, about 10 minutes. Set aside, covered, in warm place.

Melt butter in frying pan over high heat. Cook pork until browned on both sides, about 6 minutes. Season to taste with salt and pepper. Remove from pan and set aside, covered, in warm place.

Add wine and stock to pan and simmer until sauce is slightly reduced, 3–4 minutes. Add grapes and simmer until grapes are just softened, about 2 minutes.

For each serving, place two pork pieces on brioche slices. Spoon grapes and sauce over top.

Serves 4

ESCALLOPS OF PORK WITH PURPLE GRAPES

Spicy citrus-pickled shrimp

2 lb (1 kg) cooked medium shrimp (prawns),
  peeled and deveined

1 lime, thinly sliced

1 lemon, thinly sliced

1 small Spanish (purple) onion, halved and thinly
  sliced

1 tablespoon drained capers

4 bay leaves

$^{1}/_{2}$ cup (4 fl oz/125 ml) olive oil

2 tablespoons lime juice

2 tablespoons red wine vinegar

salt and freshly ground pepper

Place shrimp in large glass or ceramic bowl. Add lime and lemon slices, onion, capers and bay leaves and stir gently to combine. Combine olive oil, lime juice and vinegar in small bowl. Season to taste with salt and pepper. Pour over prawns and refrigerate, covered, stirring occasionally, about 3 hours.

Serve chilled. Accompany with green salad and bread to soak up dressing.

Serves 4

SPICY CITRUS-PICKLED SHRIMP

Salmon fillets with mango salad and basil oil

2 cups (2 oz/60 g) fresh basil leaves

$^1/_2$ cup (4 fl oz/125 ml) olive oil plus 1 tablespoon

1 mango (about 12 oz/375 g), peeled, pitted and diced

1 English (hothouse) cucumber, diced

2 tomatoes, diced

2 tablespoons lime juice

salt and freshly ground pepper

4 pieces salmon fillet (about 250 g/8 oz each), skin removed

mixed salad greens, such as arugula, baby spinach, baby beet (beetroot) greens and mizuna

Place all but four basil leaves in food processor and process until very finely chopped. Add $^1/_2$ cup (4 fl oz/125 ml) oil and process 30 seconds. Transfer to bowl, cover and allow to stand at room temperature 3–4 hours so basil infuses oil. Strain oil through fine sieve and discard basil leaves.

Combine mango, cucumber and tomatoes in bowl and stir in lime juice. Add $^1/_4$ cup (2 fl oz/60 ml) basil oil and season to taste with salt and pepper.

Press basil leaf on top of each salmon fillet. Heat 1 tablespoon olive oil in large frying pan over medium heat. Cook salmon fillets, top side first, 3–4 minutes (5–6 for well done). Season with salt and pepper. Turn and cook on second side.

Serve each fillet on bed of salad greens. Top with mango salad and drizzle with remaining basil oil.

Serves 4

SALMON FILLETS WITH MANGO SALAD AND BASIL OIL

Green papaya and butternut squash salad

2 tablespoons olive oil

1 butternut squash (pumpkin) (about 1 lb/500 g), peeled and cut into 1½ in (4-cm) pieces

1 large green papaya (about 2 lb/1 kg), peeled, seeded and grated

1 small Spanish (purple) onion, thinly sliced

¼ cup (⅓ oz/10 g) small fresh mint leaves or chopped fresh mint

¼ cup (13 oz/10 g) fresh cilantro (fresh coriander) leaves

½ cup (4 fl oz/125 ml) coconut milk

2 tablespoons lime juice

1 tablespoon fish sauce or soy sauce

1 small red chili pepper, finely chopped

Preheat oven to 350°F (180°C/Gas 4). Drizzle oil in baking pan. Add squash pieces and turn to coat with oil. Bake until tender and golden, 40–45 minutes.

Place squash pieces in large bowl and stir in papaya, onion, mint and cilantro.

Combine the remaining ingredients in small bowl. Pour over salad and gently stir to combine.

Serve at room temperature as accompaniment to broiled (grilled) or barbecued meat, poultry or seafood, or as part of Thai-style banquet.

Serves 4

Kiwifruit, cucumber, orange and cashew salad

4 kiwifruit (Chinese gooseberries), peeled and thinly sliced

1 large English (hothouse) cucumber, sliced

1 orange, peeled, sliced and seeds removed

½ cup (2 oz/60 g) toasted cashew nuts

FOR DRESSING

2 tablespoons balsamic vinegar

¼ cup (2 fl oz/60 ml) extra virgin olive oil

1 teaspoon Dijon mustard

salt and freshly ground pepper

Layer kiwifruit, cucumber and oranges slices on platter. To make dressing, combine all ingredients in small bowl. Season to taste with salt and pepper.

Pour dressing over salad. Sprinkle with toasted cashews and serve immediately as an accompaniment to spicy Moroccan or Thai dishes or barbecued seafood or chicken.

Serves 4

GREEN PAPAYA AND BUTTERNUT SQUASH SALAD

Mango and red bell pepper salsa

1 mango (about 12 oz/375 g), peeled, pitted and finely diced

1 small red bell pepper (capsicum), seeds and membranes removed and finely diced

1 small red chili pepper, thinly sliced

$^{1}/_{4}$ cup (2 fl oz/60 ml) lime juice

2 tablespoons finely chopped fresh cilantro (fresh coriander)

Combine all ingredients in bowl. Let stand, covered, at room temperature for 1 hour to allow flavors to combine. If not using immediately, refrigerate until ready to serve.

Serve with chilled oysters or sliced smoked salmon and thin slices of avocado on crisp toasted baguette slices. Salsa also makes good accompaniment to grilled chicken.

Makes 1$^{1}/_{4}$ cups (12 fl oz/375 g)

Tropical fruit salad with lime syrup

1 small pineapple (about 1$^{1}/_{2}$ lb/750 g), peeled, cored and cut into 1$^{1}/_{4}$-in (3-cm) pieces

2 mangoes (about 1$^{1}/_{2}$ lb/750 g), peeled, pitted and sliced

1 small red papaya (about 1$^{1}/_{4}$ lb/625 g), peeled, seeded and cut into 1$^{1}/_{4}$-in (3-cm) pieces

4 passion fruit, peeled and seeded

1 tablespoon finely chopped candied (crystallized) ginger

2 bananas, peeled and sliced

FOR SYRUP

$^{1}/_{4}$ cup (2 fl oz/60 ml) lime juice

2 tablespoons dark rum

$^{1}/_{4}$ cup (1$^{3}/_{4}$ oz/50 g) superfine (caster) sugar

Combine all ingredients except bananas in large serving bowl.

To make syrup, combine all ingredients in small saucepan over low heat. Cook for 3–4 minutes, stirring to dissolve sugar. Cover and cool completely in refrigerator before using.

To serve, pour syrup over fruit and top with banana slices.

Serves 6 to 8

MANGO AND RED BELL PEPPER SALSA

Apple and date cake

2 tart green apples, peeled, cored and cut into
$^3/_4$-in (2-cm) chunks

1 cup (5$^3/_4$ oz/175 g) chopped pitted dates

1 teaspoon baking soda (bicarbonate of soda)

1 cup (8 fl oz/250 ml) boiling water

4 oz (125 g) unsalted butter

1 cup (6$^1/_2$ oz/200 g) superfine (caster) sugar

1 egg

1 teaspoon vanilla extract (essence)

1$^1/_2$ (7$^1/_4$ oz/225 g) cups all-purpose (plain) flour,
sifted

FOR TOPPING

2 oz (60 g) unsalted butter

2 tablespoons milk

$^1/_2$ cup (33/4 oz/110 g) packed brown sugar

$^1/_2$ cup (23/4 oz/80 g) unsweetened shredded
(desiccated) coconut

Preheat oven to 350°F (180°C/Gas 4). Grease 9-inch (23-cm) round cake pan with removable sides and line with parchment (baking paper).

Place apples, dates and baking soda in bowl and pour in boiling water. Let stand until cool.

Beat butter and sugar in a bowl until pale. Beat in egg and vanilla. Fold in flour alternately with apple mixture. Spread in pan and bake 45 minutes.

Meanwhile, to make topping, place all ingredients in saucepan over low heat. Stir until butter is melted, and sugar is dissolved and mixture is combined, about 5 minutes.

Remove cake from oven and spread evenly with topping. Return to oven and bake until topping is golden and skewer inserted in middle of cake comes out clean, about 15 minutes. Allow cake to cool in pan completely before carefully removing sides of pan and transferring cake to plate to serve.

Serves 8–10

APPLE AND DATE CAKE

Apple pie

FOR PASTRY

2 cups (10 oz/300 g) all-purpose (plain) flour

5 oz (150 g) chilled unsalted butter, cut into small pieces

2 tablespoons superfine (caster) sugar

2 tablespoons ice water

1 egg yolk

FOR FILLING

4 oz (125 g) butter

1 cup (7¹/₄ oz/225 g) packed brown sugar

2 tablespoons lemon juice

2 tablespoons finely grated lemon zest

5 tart green apples, peeled, cored and cut into eighths

heavy (double) cream, whipped, for garnish

To make pastry, place flour, butter and sugar in food processor and process until mixture resembles fine bread crumbs. Lightly whisk together water and egg yolk and add to flour mixture. Process just until mixture starts to come together. Remove from processor and gently knead so mixture forms mass. Pat into disk, wrap in plastic wrap and refrigerate 30 minutes.

Divide pastry into two pieces, one twice the size of the other. Refrigerate smaller piece. Roll out larger piece on lightly floured surface to fit 10-inch (25-cm) tart pan with removable bottom. Line with pastry, trim edges and refrigerate 30 minutes. Preheat oven to 400°F (200°C/Gas 6). Line pastry with parchment (baking paper) and cover with dried beans or rice. Bake 20 minutes, then remove beans or rice and paper. Return to oven and bake until golden, about 5 minutes. Set aside to cool slightly.

To make filling, melt butter with sugar in large frying pan over a low heat, stirring to dissolve sugar. Stir in lemon juice and zest. Add apples and simmer until soft, about 20 minutes. Set aside to cool. Using slotted spoon, transfer apples to pastry shell, allowing as much liquid as possible to drain from each spoonful.

Preheat oven to 350°F (180°C/Gas 4). Roll out remaining pastry and cut into strips. Place over apple mixture in lattice pattern. Bake until pastry is crisp and golden, about 20 minutes.

Meanwhile, pour remaining apple cooking juices in small pan over medium heat. Boil until thick and syrupy, 3–4 minutes. Serve apple pie warm, garnished with apple syrup and whipped cream.

Serves 8–10

Blueberry cheesecakes

4 oz (125 g) graham crackers or other
   plain sweet cookies

$2^3/4$ oz (80 g) unsalted butter,
   melted

1 lb (500 g) ricotta cheese

1 lb (500 g) cream cheese

2 tablespoons finely grated lemon
   zest

$2/3$ cup (4 oz/125 g) superfine
   (caster) sugar

3 eggs

$1^1/2$ cups (8 oz/250 g) blueberries

Place graham crackers or cookies in food processor and process until fine. Place in bowl and stir in butter until thoroughly combined. Press $1^1/2$ tablespoons crumb mixture into bottom of eight 4-inch (10-cm) tart pans with removable bottoms. Refrigerate 30 minutes.

Preheat oven to 350°F (180°C/Gas 4). Place ricotta, cream cheese, lemon zest and sugar in food processor and process until smooth or put in bowl and beat with electric mixer until smooth. Add eggs and process or beat until combined.

    Divide filling evenly among tart pans. Evenly distribute berries over tops. Bake until middle of each cheesecake is firm, about 25 minutes. Allow to cool completely. Remove sides and bottom of pans and serve.

Makes 8

Blueberry and almond mini muffins

1 cup (4 oz/125 g) ground almonds

$1/3$ cup (2 oz/60 g) all-purpose
   (plain) flour, sifted

$1^1/2$ cups ($6^1/2$ oz/200 g)
   confectioners' (icing) sugar, sifted

6 egg whites, lightly beaten

6 oz (180 g) unsalted butter, melted

$3/4$ cup (4 oz/125 g) blueberries

confectioners' (icing) sugar
   (optional), for garnish

Preheat oven to 425°F (220°C/Gas 7). Grease two 12-cup mini muffin pans or line cups with paper liners.

Combine almonds, flour and $1^1/2$ cups ($6^1/2$ oz/200 g) sugar in large bowl and stir in egg whites alternately with melted butter. Gently fold in blueberries.

Spoon into pans. Bake for 7 minutes. Reduce heat to 400°F (200°C/Gas 6) and bake until golden, 7 to 10 minutes. Allow muffins to cool slightly in pans before turning onto wire rack to cool completely.

    To serve, dust with confectioners' sugar if desired.

Makes 24

BLUEBERRY CHEESECAKES

Kiwifruit sponge cake

4 eggs

$^1/_2$ cup ($3^1/_4$ oz/110 g) superfine (caster) sugar

1 cup (5 oz/150 g) all-purpose, (plain) flour, sifted

$^1/_4$ teaspoon salt

2 oz (60 g) unsalted butter, melted and cooled

$1^1/_{2}$ cups (12 fl oz/375 ml) heavy (double) cream, whipped

5 kiwifruit (Chinese gooseberries), peeled and thinly sliced

Preheat oven to 350°F (180°C/Gas 4). Grease 8-inch (20-cm) round or square cake pan and line with parchment (baking paper).

Combine eggs and sugar in bowl. Using electric mixer, beat until pale and thick, 5–7 minutes. Fold in flour and salt in two batches, folding in butter with last batch. Transfer prepared pan and bake until cake feels firm in middle, 25–30 minutes. Allow cake to cool in pan 5 minutes before turning onto wire rack to cool completely.

When cake is completely cool, cut horizontally into four even layers. Spread bottom layer with one-fourth of cream. Top with layer of kiwifruit slices. Repeat layers of cake, whipped cream and kiwifruit.

Serve cake immediately or store, covered, in refrigerator until ready to serve.

Serves 8–10

KIWIFRUIT SPONGE CAKE

Lemon tart

FOR PASTRY

1$\frac{1}{2}$ cups (7$\frac{1}{4}$ oz/225 g) all-purpose (plain) flour

6 oz (180 g) unsalted butter

1 tablespoon superfine (caster) sugar

2 tablespoons ice water

1 egg yolk

FOR FILLING

$\frac{2}{3}$ cup (5 fl oz/150 ml) lemon juice

$\frac{3}{4}$ cup (5 oz/150 g) superfine (caster) sugar

$\frac{1}{4}$ cup (2 fl oz/60 ml) heavy (double) cream

5 eggs

2 tablespoons confectioners' (icing) sugar (optional), for garnish

To make pastry, place flour, butter and sugar in food processor and process until mixture resembles fine bread crumbs. Lightly whisk together water and egg yolk and add to flour mixture. Process just until mixture starts to come together. Remove from processor and gently knead so mixture forms mass. Pat into disk, wrap in plastic wrap and refrigerate 30 minutes.

Roll out pastry to fit 12-inch (30-cm) round tart pan with removable bottom. Line pan with pastry, trim edges and refrigerate 30 minutes. Preheat oven to 400°F (200°C/Gas 6). Line pastry with parchment (baking paper) and cover with dried beans or rice. Bake 25 minutes, then remove beans or rice and paper. Return to oven and bake until golden, about 10 minutes. Set aside to cool slightly. Reduce heat to 350°F (180°C/Gas 4).

To make filling, combine lemon juice, superfine sugar and cream in bowl and whisk until combined. Add eggs, one at a time, whisking well after each addition. Pour into pastry shell. Bake until tart feels set in middle, about 20 minutes. Allow tart to cool in pan before carefully removing sides of pan and transferring tart to plate.

Serve dusted with confectioners' sugar, if desired.

LEMON TART

Old-fashioned lemon cake

FOR CAKE

10 oz (300 g) unsalted butter

1 1/2 cups (10 oz/300 g) superfine (caster) sugar

6 eggs

2 1/4 cups (11 oz/330 g) self-rising flour, sifted

2/3 cup (3 1/4 oz/100 g) all-purpose (plain) flour, sifted

1/3 cup (2 1/2 fl oz/75 ml) milk

3 tablespoons finely grated lemon zest

FOR SYRUP

zest of 3 lemons, cut into thin strips

2/3 cup (5 fl oz/150 ml) lemon juice

1/4 cup (2 fl oz/60 ml) water

3/4 cup (5 oz/150 g) superfine (caster) sugar

To make cake, preheat oven to 350°F (180°C/Gas 4). Grease 9-inch (23-cm) bundt pan.

Using electric mixer, beat butter and sugar in large bowl just until combined. Add eggs, flours, milk and lemon zest and beat on low speed until combined. Then beat on high speed until batter is light and creamy, about 5 minutes.

Spread in prepared pan. Bake until skewer inserted in middle of cake comes out clean, about 50 minutes. Allow cake to cool in pan 5 minutes before turning onto wire rack to cool completely.

To make syrup, place zest strips in bowl and add boiling water to cover. Let stand 10 minutes, then drain. Combine zest and remaining ingredients in small saucepan over low heat, stirring to dissolve sugar. Raise heat, bring to boil and boil until syrup is thickened and zest is translucent, 5–7 minutes.

Pierce top of cake thoroughly with skewer. Brush with syrup, allowing cake to absorb syrup. Decorate top with lemon zest strips and serve.

Serves 8 to 10

Orange cake with plum glaze

FOR CAKE

8 oz (250 g) unsalted butter

2 cups (13 oz/400 g) superfine (caster) sugar

6 eggs

3 cups (15 oz/470 g) all-purpose (plain) flour, sifted

1 cup (8 oz/250 g) sour cream

1 tablespoon orange juice

2 tablespoons finely grated orange zest

FOR GLAZE

1 cup (6 1/2 oz/200 g) superfine (caster) sugar

1 1/2 cups (12 fl oz/375 ml) water

10 red-fleshed plums, cut around pit and left whole

To make cake, preheat oven to 350°F (180°C/Gas 4). Grease 10-inch (25-cm) bundt pan.

Cream butter and sugar in bowl using electric mixer. Beat in eggs, one at a time, beating well after each addition. Fold in flour alternately with sour cream, adding orange juice and zest with last batch of flour.

Pour into prepared pan and bake until skewer inserted in middle of cake comes out clean, about 40 minutes. Let cool in pan slightly before turning onto wire rack to cool completely.

Meanwhile, to make glaze, combine sugar and water in saucepan over low heat, stirring to dissolve sugar, about 4 minutes. Raise heat, bring to boil, add plums and simmer until tender, about 5 minutes. Pour plums and liquid into bowl. Let stand at least 1 hour, covered, to allow glaze to turn red. When cool, slip peels from plums and remove pits.

Pierce top of cake thoroughly with skewer. Brush with plum glaze, allowing cake to absorb glaze. Brush sides of cake so color is uniform.

Accompany each serving of cake with one plum.

Serves 10

OLD-FASHIONED LEMON CAKE

Chocolate pear tartlets

FOR PASTRY

1 1/2 cups (7 1/4 oz/225 g) all-purpose (plain) flour

6 oz (180 g) chilled unsalted butter, cut into small
    pieces

1 tablespoon superfine (caster) sugar

2 tablespoons ice water

1 egg yolk

FOR FILLING

1 cup (7 oz/220 g) superfine (caster) sugar

2 cups (16 fl oz/500 ml) water

2 Packham or Anjou pears, peeled, cored and
    quartered

13 oz (400 g) semisweet dark chocolate

5 1/4 oz (160 g) unsalted butter

6 egg yolks

1 egg

1/2 cup (3 3/4 oz/110 g) superfine (caster) sugar

1 tablespoon dark rum or brandy

2 tablespoons unsweetened cocoa powder
    (optional), for garnish

To make pastry, place flour, butter and sugar in food processor and process until mixture resembles fine bread crumbs. Lightly whisk together water and egg yolk and add to flour mixture. Process just until mixture starts to come together. Remove from processor and gently knead so mixture forms a mass. Pat into disk, wrap in plastic wrap and refrigerate 30 minutes.

Preheat oven to 350°F (180°C/Gas 4). Roll out pastry on lightly floured surface and line eight 4-inch (10-cm) tart pans or one 12-inch (30-cm) tart pan with removable bottom. Line pastry with parchment (baking paper) and cover with dried beans or rice. Bake 20 minutes, then remove beans or rice and paper. Return to oven and bake until golden, 5 minutes. Set aside to cool for 10 minutes.

Meanwhile, to make filling, combine 1/2 cup sugar (31/2 oz/110 g)and water in saucepan over low heat, stirring to dissolve sugar, about 3 minutes. Raise heat, bring to boil, add pears and simmer until pears are tender and translucent, 7–10 minutes. Remove pears with slotted spoon and set aside, covered, to cool. When cool, slice each pear quarter lengthwise into five thin slices, leaving slices together in shape of pear quarter.

Combine chocolate and butter in top of double boiler or metal bowl set over small saucepan of water. Cook over simmering water, stirring, until chocolate is melted and combined with butter. In bowl, whisk together egg yolks, egg and sugar until thick and pale, 5–7 minutes. Stir into chocolate mixture. Stir in rum or brandy.

Arrange pear slices, fanning them out, on each tart shell or on large pastry shell. Cover evenly with chocolate mixture. Bake until filling is firm in middle, about 25 minutes. Allow to cool completely. Remove sides and bottom of tart pans and serve. Dust with cocoa if desired.

Makes 8

CHOCOLATE PEAR TARTLETS

Upside-down pear gingerbread

FOR TOPPING

1 cup (6¹/₂ oz/200 g) superfine (caster) sugar

3 cups (24 fl oz/750 ml) water

3 Packham or Anjou pears, peeled, cored and halved

2 oz (60 g) unsalted butter

¹/₂ cup (3³/₄ oz/110 g) packed brown sugar

FOR GINGERBREAD

³/₄ cup (3³/₄ oz/110 g) all-purpose (plain) flour

¹/₂ teaspoon baking soda (bicarbonate of soda)

¹/₄ teaspoon salt

2 teaspoons ground cinnamon

1 teaspoon ground ginger

1 egg, beaten

³/₄ cup (5¹/₂ oz/165 g) packed brown sugar

¹/₄ cup (3 oz/90 g) maple syrup (golden syrup)

¹/₂ cup (4 oz/125 g) sour cream

2 oz (60 g) unsalted butter, melted and cooled

To make topping, combine superfine sugar and water in saucepan over low heat, stirring to dissolve sugar. Raise heat and bring to boil. Reduce heat to medium, add pear halves and cook, turning occasionally, until pears are tender, about 10 minutes. Using slotted spoon, remove pears and set aside, covered, to cool. Discard syrup.

Melt butter in small saucepan over low heat and add brown sugar, stirring until sugar is melted and mixture is combined, 1–2 minutes. Pour into 9-inch (23-cm) round cake pan. Arrange pears, cut side down, over top.

To make gingerbread, preheat oven to 350°F (180°C/Gas 4). Sift flour, baking soda, salt and spices into large bowl. Place remaining ingredients in another bowl and stir to combine. Stir into flour and spice mixture until thoroughly combined. Pour over pears. Bake until skewer inserted in middle comes out clean, 55–60 minutes. Allow to cool in pan 10 minutes before turning onto serving plate. Serve warm or cold.

Serves 8–10

UPSIDE-DOWN PEAR GINGERBREAD

Warm banana cake with caramel bananas

FOR CAKE

4 oz (125 g) unsalted butter

1¹/₂ cups (9¹/₄ oz/285 g) superfine (caster) sugar

2 eggs

1 cup (8 oz/250 g) mashed banana

1 teaspoon vanilla extract (essence)

2³/₄ cups (14¹/₄ oz/450 g) all-purpose (plain) flour

1 teaspoon baking soda (bicarbonate of soda)

¹/₂ cup (4 fl oz/125 ml) buttermilk

FOR CARAMEL BANANAS

¹/₂ cup (3³/₄ oz/110 g) superfine (caster) sugar

¹/₂ cup (4 fl oz/125 ml) water

1 cup (8 fl oz/250 ml) heavy (double) cream

4 bananas, peeled and sliced

Grease 8-in (20-cm) round cake pan with removable sides. Preheat oven to 350°F (180°C/Gas 4).

Cream butter and sugar with electric mixer. Add eggs, one at a time, beating after each addition. Beat in banana and vanilla. Sift dry ingredients into bowl. Stir into egg mixture alternately with buttermilk. Spoon into prepared pan and bake until skewer inserted in middle comes out clean, about 45 minutes. Cool in pan for 5 minutes before turning onto wire rack. Cake can be made ahead and heated for 1 minute, covered, on high power in microwave oven.

Meanwhile, to make caramel bananas, combine sugar and water in small saucepan over low heat and cook, stirring to dissolve sugar, about 2 minutes. Raise heat, bring to boil and boil without stirring until mixture just turns golden, about 7 minutes. Remove from heat and cool slightly, about 1 minute. Stir in cream and bananas.

To serve, top slices of warm cake with caramel bananas.

Serves 8

WARM BANANA CAKE WITH CARAMEL BANANAS

Strawberry shortcakes

1¹/₂ cups (7¹/₄ oz/225 g) all-purpose (plain) flour

5 oz (150 g) unsalted butter, cut into small pieces

¹/₂ cup (2¹/₂ oz/75 g) confectioners' (icing) sugar

3 egg yolks

1 teaspoon vanilla extract (essence)

1¹/₂ cups (12 fl oz/375 ml) heavy (double) cream

2 tablespoons superfine (caster) sugar

2 cups (1 lb/500 g) hulled (stemmed) strawberries

2 tablespoons confectioners' (icing) sugar, for garnish

Sift flour into bowl and make well in middle. Put butter, 1/2 cup (2 1/2 oz/75 g) confectioners' sugar, egg yolks and vanilla in well. Using fork, gradually stir ingredients in well, incorporating flour, until smooth paste has formed. Gently knead to thoroughly combine. Set in cool place, covered, for 1 hour.

Preheat oven to 350°F (180°C/Gas 4). Divide pastry into two equal portions and pat each into 9-inch (23-cm) disk about 1/2 inch (12 mm) thick. Place on baking sheet and bake until golden, 15–20 minutes. Transfer to wire rack to cool. While still warm, cut one disk into eight sections. Allow to cool completely.

Meanwhile, combine cream and superfine sugar and whip until soft peaks form. Place strawberries in large bowl and fold in cream. Refrigerate, covered, until ready to use.

To serve, place whole shortcake disk on plate and top with strawberries and cream. Place eight shortcake sections on top or to side. Dust with confectioners' sugar.

Serves 8

STRAWBERRY SHORTCAKES

Pears in black currant syrup

1¹/₂ cups (12 fl oz/375 ml) water

1 cup (8 fl oz/250 ml) black currant syrup

4 Packham or Anjou pears, peeled

Place water and black currant syrup in large saucepan over medium-high heat and bring to boil. Add pears, reduce heat and simmer until tender, about 30 minutes. Remove pears with slotted spoon and place in bowl. Bring poaching liquid to boil and cook until reduced by half, about 10 minutes.

Serve pears warm with warm syrup spooned over top.

Serves 4

Variation

Poached peaches also make a delightful dessert. Combine 2 cups water and ¹/₄ cup sugar and stir over low heat to dissolve sugar. Bring to boil and reduce heat to a steady simmer. Add peaches (1 per person) and simmer for 15 minutes. Remove with slotted spoon and set aside.

Bring syrup back to boil and boil until reduced by half, about 5 minutes. Serve whole, warm peaches with syrup and cream if desired.

PEARS IN BLACK CURRANT SYRUP

Peaches with vanilla custard

1 cup (6 1/2 oz/200 g) superfine (caster) sugar

1 cup (8 fl oz/250 ml) dry white wine

1 1/2 cups (12 fl oz/375 ml) water

4 peaches

FOR CUSTARD

4 egg yolks

1/3 cup (2 oz/60 g) superfine (caster) sugar

1 cup (8 fl oz/250 ml) heavy (double) cream

Place sugar, wine and water in saucepan over low heat and cook, stirring to dissolve sugar, about 2 minutes. Raise heat, bring to boil, reduce heat to medium, add peaches and simmer until tender, about 15 minutes. Remove peaches with slotted spoon and place in bowl to cool slightly. Remove peels. Halve and remove pits if desired. Bring poaching liquid to boil and cook until reduced by half, about 10 minutes. Pour over peaches, cover and set aside.

Peaches can be poached two days in advance and stored, covered, in refrigerator. Remove from refrigerator 1 hour before serving to bring to room temperature.

To make custard, combine egg yolks and sugar in top part of double boiler or in metal bowl set over saucepan half filled with water. Whisk until pale and thick, 4–5 minutes. Place over simmering water and stir in cream. Cook, stirring constantly, until custard thickens and coats back of spoon, 7–10 minutes.

To serve, place peaches in individual bowls. Accompany with custard, at room temperature or chilled. Spoon poaching liquid over top.

Serves 4

PEACHES WITH VANILLA CUSTARD

Plums with Bavarian cream

1 cup (6½ oz/200 g) superfine (caster) sugar

3 cups (24 fl oz/750 ml) water

12 red-fleshed plums, cut around pit and left whole

FOR BAVARIAN CREAM

1 teaspoon vegetable oil

1 tablespoon unflavored gelatin

¼ cup (2 fl oz/60 ml) boiling water

¾ (6 fl oz/180 ml) milk

⅔ cup (4 oz/125 g) superfine (caster) sugar

4 egg yolks

1 cup (8 fl oz/250 ml) heavy (double) cream, whipped

Combine sugar and water in saucepan over low heat and cook, stirring to dissolve sugar, 2–3 minutes. Raise heat, bring to boil, reduce heat to medium and add plums. Poach until plums are tender and start to pull away from pits, 7–10 minutes. Remove plums with slotted spoon and place in bowl to cool slightly. Halve each plum, remove pit and slip off peel. Bring poaching liquid to boil and cook until reduced by half, about 10 minutes. Pour over plums. Plums can be poached three to four days in advance and stored, covered, in refrigerator.

To make Bavarian cream, lightly brush six ⅔ cup (5 fl oz/150 ml) metal molds with oil. Sprinkle gelatin over boiling water and stir with fork until completely dissolved. Combine milk and sugar in small saucepan over low heat and cook, stirring to dissolve sugar, about 2 minutes. Place egg yolks in separate saucepan and pour in warm milk. Whisk to combine. Place mixture over low heat and cook, stirring constantly, until it thickens and coats back of spoon, 7–10 minutes. Pour into bowl and, using electric mixer, beat in dissolved gelatin until completely incorporated and cream begins to cool, 3–4 minutes. Fold in whipped cream and pour into molds. Refrigerate, covered, at least 3–4 hours or overnight.

To serve, immerse each mold briefly in warm water and invert onto plate. Gently tap to free cream from mold. Bring plums to room temperature or serve cold. Spoon two plums and some of syrup on each plate.

Serves 6

PLUMS WITH BAVARIAN CREAM

Blackberry sauce

1/4 cup (1 3/4 oz/50 g) superfine (caster) sugar, or more as needed

1/2 cup (4 fl oz/125 ml) water

1 tablespoon orange flower water

2 cups (1 lb/500 g) blackberries

Combine sugar, water and orange flower water in saucepan over low heat, stirring to dissolve sugar. Raise heat, bring to boil and cook 3 minutes. Reduce heat to low and add blackberries. Gently stir until heated through, about 1 minute. Taste and add more sugar, 1 teaspoon at a time, until sauce is to your liking. Serve warm or at room temperature. Sauce can be refrigerated for two days.

Makes 3 cups (24 fl oz/750 ml)

Hints

Serve with slices of your favorite cake or with ice cream. The sauce is also good with sliced peaches, nectarines, apricots and plums, as well as halved figs. If orange flower water is not available, substitute 2 tablespoons orange-flavored liqueur or 1 tablespoon finely grated orange zest.

BLACKBERRY SAUCE

Mango and passion fruit sauce

3 mangoes (about 2¹/₂ lb/1.1 kg), peeled, pitted and sliced

6 passion fruit, peeled and seeded

2 tablespoons superfine (caster) sugar

Serve over a mixed fruit salad or over ice cream, or with slices of lemon sponge cake.

Place all ingredients in small saucepan over low heat and cook, stirring to dissolve sugar, about 2 minutes. Raise heat and bring to boil. Remove from heat and cool slightly before serving. Sauce can be refrigerated for one day.

Makes 4 cups (32 fl oz/1 L)

Gingered litchi sauce

¹/₄ cup (2 fl oz/60 ml) lime juice

¹/₃ cup (2 oz/60 g) superfine (caster) sugar

1 piece fresh ginger (about 2 in/5 cm), peeled and sliced

3 kaffir lime leaves or 1 lime, sliced

¹/₄ cup (¹/₂ oz/10 g) fresh mint leaves

16 litchis (lychees), peeled, halved and pitted

Pair this sauce with chilled papaya, mango or pineapple slices or with fruit sorbets such as lemon or melon. If fresh litchis are unavailable, canned ones may be used.

Combine lime juice, sugar and ginger in small saucepan over low heat and cook, stirring to dissolve sugar, about 1 minute. Pour lime syrup into small container, cover and refrigerate until cold.

Place lime syrup in serving bowl and add remaining ingredients. Stir to combine, cover and refrigerate 1 hour to allow flavors to blend. Remove ginger pieces and kaffir lime leaves before serving. Sauce can be refrigerated for two days.

Makes 4 cups (32 fl oz/1 L)

MANGO AND PASSION FRUIT SAUCE

Bread-and-butter berry puddings

8 slices bread, crusts removed

2 oz (60 g) unsalted butter, softened

1 cup (8 oz/250 g) hulled (stemmed) strawberries,
   chopped

²/₃ cup (5 oz/150 g) raspberries

²/₃ cup (5 oz/150 g) blackberries

2 eggs

2¹/₂ cups (20 fl oz/625 ml) heavy (double) cream

¹/₂ cup (3¹/₄ oz/100 g) superfine (caster) sugar

double (heavy) cream, whipped, for garnish

2 tablespoons confectioners' (icing) sugar,
   (optional), for garnish

Preheat oven 350°F (180°C/Gas 4). Cut each slice of bread into four triangles and butter each side. Combine berries in bowl. Place 1 tablespoon berries in bottom of each of eight 6–fl oz (180-ml) ramekins. Top with triangle of bread. Repeat with another 1 tablespoon berries and bread triangle. For final layer, place two bread triangles in each ramekin with points facing up and fill with remaining berries.

Whisk eggs, cream and superfine sugar in bowl. Pour into ramekins, dividing evenly and refilling as bread absorbs mixture. Place in baking pan and add boiling water to reach halfway up sides of ramekins.

Bake until middle of each pudding feels firm to touch, about 45 minutes. Cool slightly before serving. Garnish with whipped cream and dust with confectioners' sugar if desired.

Makes 8

BREAD-AND-BUTTER BERRY PUDDINGS

Dark cherry trifle

1 package (3 oz/90 g) cherry-flavored gelatin

2 cups (1 lb/500 g) pitted, sweet dark cherries

$^1/_4$ cup (2 fl oz/60 ml) cherry brandy or
   maraschino liqueur

1 store-bought sponge cake (8 in/20 cm diameter)

FOR PASTRY CREAM

4 egg yolks

$^1/_3$ cup (2 oz/60 g) superfine (caster) sugar

$1^1/_2$ tablespoons all-purpose (plain) flour

1 cup (8 fl oz/250 ml) milk

1 teaspoon vanilla extract (essence)

1 cup (8 fl oz/250 ml) heavy (double) cream,
   whipped

Make gelatin in wide, shallow bowl according to directions on package. Chill in refrigerator until completely set, about 2 hours.

Place cherries in bowl and add brandy or liqueur. Let stand, covered, at room temperature, stirring occasionally, for 2–3 hours.

Meanwhile, to make cream, whisk egg yolks and sugar in bowl until thick and pale, 4–5 minutes. Whisk in flour. Place milk in small saucepan over very low heat and cook just until milk is warm and steam begins to rise from surface. Strain into egg yolk mixture and whisk until combined. Transfer to saucepan over low heat and cook until cream thickens and coats back of spoon, 7–10 minutes. Pour into bowl, cover with plastic wrap placed directly on surface of cream and refrigerate until cool. Fold in whipped cream.

Cut sponge cake into 16 thin slices that fit into four 1$^1/_2$-cup (12–fl oz/375-ml) serving dishes. For each serving, you will need four slices. Cut four extra pieces of cake in small triangles for decoration. Place layer of cake in bottom of each dish and top with four or five cherries, 2 tablespoons set gelatin and 2 tablespoons pastry cream. Repeat layers three more times. Top each dish with a sponge cake triangle. Refrigerate, covered, until ready to serve.

Serves 4

DARK CHERRY TRIFLE

Baked apples

4 sweet green or red apples

4 oz (125 g) very cold unsalted butter, cut into pieces

$^1/_2$ cup ($3^3/_4$ oz/110 g) packed brown sugar

$^1/_2$ cup (2 oz/60 g) walnuts

$^1/_4$ cup ($1^1/_4$ oz/40 g) unsweetened shredded (desiccated) coconut

4 dried pears (optional)

heavy (double) cream, whipped, for garnish

Preheat oven to 350°F (180°C/Gas 4). Remove peel from top half of each apple, creating an attractive design if desired; core each apple without cutting through bottom. Combine butter, brown sugar, walnuts and coconut in food processor and process until just combined. Fill cores with mixture and place in a shallow baking pan.

Bake 15 minutes. If desired, remove from oven and gently insert one dried pear into filling of each apple, being careful not to squeeze out too much filling. Bake until apples are soft, 5–10 minutes. Serve warm with whipped cream.

Serves 4

Variation

Combine $^1/_3$ cup ($1^1/_2$ oz/45 g) ground almonds, $1^1/_2$ oz (45 g) unsalted butter, $^1/_3$ cup ($2^1/_2$ oz/75 g) lightly packed brown sugar and $^1/_4$ cup ($1^1/_2$ oz/45 g) dried currants in small bowl and stir to blend. Spoon into cored apples. Press a cinnamon stick into each filled core. Bake as directed.

BAKED APPLES

Panfried pineapple

6 oz (180 g) unsalted butter

1 small pineapple (about 1½ lb/750 g), peeled, cut lengthwise into quarters, cored and thinly sliced

¾ cup (5½ oz/165 g) packed brown sugar

¼ cup (2 fl oz/60 ml) dark rum or brandy

Melt butter in large frying pan over medium heat. Add pineapple slices and cook for 1 minute. Sprinkle evenly with brown sugar and cook, turning pineapple occasionally, until sugar is melted and pineapple is translucent, 2–3 minutes. Add rum or brandy, stir to combine and cook 1 minute.

To serve, place pineapple on plates and spoon warm sauce over top.

Serves 4

Variations

Same method can be used for fresh figs. You will need 1½ lb (750 g) figs. Halve each fig and cook as directed, decreasing cooking time of 2–3 minutes to 1–2 minutes as figs soften quicker than pineapple.

Four bananas, peeled and sliced, can also be substituted for pineapple. Cook as directed, reducing cooking time of 2–3 minutes to 1–2 minutes. To serve, sprinkle with toasted unsweetened shredded (desiccated) coconut if desired.

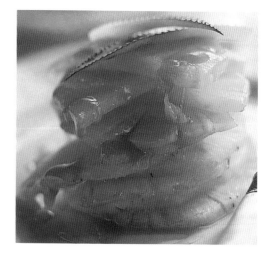

PANFRIED PINEAPPLE

Brandied pear, cherry and apricot crumble

FOR FRUIT

1 cup (6^1/$_2$ oz/200 g) superfine (caster) sugar

3 cups (24 fl oz/750 ml) water

2 Bosc or Packham pears, peeled, cored and
  quartered

8 apricots

1 cup (8 oz/250 g) sweet yellow or red cherries
  with stems intact

^{1}/$_2$ cup (4 fl oz/125 ml) brandy

FOR CRUMBLE

1 cup (5 oz/150 g) all-purpose (plain) flour

2^3/$_4$ oz (80 g) very cold unsalted butter

^{1}/$_2$ cup (3^3/$_4$ oz/110 g) packed brown sugar

^{1}/$_2$ cup (2^1/$_2$ oz/75 g) rolled oats

^{3}/$_4$ cup (3 oz/90 g) walnuts

To make fruit, combine sugar and water in saucepan over low heat and cook, stirring to dissolve sugar, 3–4 minutes. Raise heat and bring to boil. Add pear quarters and apricots, reduce heat and simmer until tender, about 10 minutes. Add cherries and simmer 2–3 minutes. Remove fruit with slotted spoon and place in bowl. Bring poaching liquid to boil and cook until reduced by half and syrupy, about 10 minutes. Remove from heat and stir in brandy. Allow to cool slightly, cover and refrigerate 48 hours. Cover and refrigerate fruit separately.

To make crumble, place all ingredients in food processor and process just until mixture resembles coarse bread crumbs. Do not overprocess or mixture will stick together. Use immediately or refrigerate, covered, until ready to use.

Preheat oven to 350°F (180°C/Gas 4). Place fruit and 1 cup (8 fl oz/250 ml) reduced poaching liquid in 6–8-cup (48–64–fl oz/ 1^1/2–2-L) baking dish. Sprinkle evenly with crumble mixture. Bake until crumble is crisp and golden, 20–25 minutes. Serve warm.

Serves 4

BRANDIED PEAR, CHERRY AND APRICOT CRUMBLE

Strawberries and mangoes with zabaglione

1 1/2 cups (12 oz/375 g) hulled (stemmed) strawberries, halved

2 mangoes (about 1 1/2 lb/750 g), peeled, pitted and sliced

FOR ZABAGLIONE

4 egg yolks

1/4 cup (1 1/2 oz/45 g) superfine (caster) sugar

1/4 cup (2 fl oz/60 ml) orange-flavored liqueur

Combine strawberries and mango slices in bowl. Store, covered, in refrigerator until serving.

To make zabaglione, place all ingredients in top of double boiler or in metal bowl set over saucepan one-third filled with water. Whisk, off heat, until combined. Place over simmering water and continue to whisk until pale and fluffy, about 5 minutes.

Spoon fruit into individual dishes. Top with zabaglione and serve immediately.

Serves 4

Strawberries in raspberry cream

2 cups (1 lb/500 g) hulled (stemmed) strawberries

2 tablespoons superfine (caster) sugar

1/4 cup (2 fl oz/60 ml) orange juice

2 tablespoons kirsch

FOR RASPBERRY CREAM

1 cup (8 oz/250 g) raspberries

1/4 cup (1 oz/30 g) confectioners' (icing) sugar

1 cup (8 fl oz/250 ml) heavy (double) cream, lightly whipped

Place strawberries in serving bowl and dust with sugar. Add orange juice and kirsch and stir to combine. Cover and refrigerate while preparing raspberry cream.

To make raspberry cream, place raspberries in food processor or blender and process until smooth. Strain to remove as many seeds as possible. Stir in sugar. Fold in cream and refrigerate, covered, until ready to serve.

Serve strawberries in dishes topped with raspberry cream.

Serves 4

STRAWBERRIES AND MANGOES WITH ZABAGLIONE

Watermelon gelatin

4 raspberry-flavored teabags

4½ cups (36 fl oz/1.1 L) boiling water

1 cup (6½ oz/200 g) superfine (castor) sugar

2 teaspoons lime juice

1 tablespoon unflavored gelatin

2 cups (12 oz/375 g) seedless cubed watermelon

star-shaped watermelon pieces (optional), for
   garnish

Place teabags in bowl and steep in 4 cups (32 fl oz/1 L) boiling water for 5 minutes. Remove teabags. Add sugar and lime juice and stir to dissolve sugar. Sprinkle gelatin over ½ cup (4 fl oz/100 ml) boiling water and stir to dissolve. Add to tea mixture and stir to combine.

Divide the watermelon cubes among eight 1-cup (8–fl oz/250-ml) molds. Pour in tea mixture, dividing evenly. Decorate with watermelon stars, if desired. Refrigerate overnight or until set.

Serves 8

WATERMELON GELATIN

Whiskey oranges

6 oranges, peeled and pith removed

1 cup (8 fl oz/250 ml) water

$^3/_4$ cup (5 oz/150 g) superfine (caster) sugar

$^1/_3$ cup (2$^3/_4$ fl oz/80 ml) whiskey

FOR TOFFEE SHARDS

$^1/_2$ teaspoon vegetable oil

1 cup (6$^1/_2$ oz/200 g) superfine (caster) sugar

1 cup (8 fl oz/250 ml) water

Slice each orange horizontally into eight slices, removing any seeds, and reassemble into whole. Place in deep baking dish. Combine water and sugar in saucepan over low heat, stirring to dissolve sugar. Raise heat, bring to boil and cook, without stirring, until mixture just starts to turn golden, 7–8 minutes. Remove from heat and stir in whiskey, being careful not to burn your hand as mixture will bubble up. Pour over oranges and let stand, covered, at room temperature 1 hour, to combine flavors.

To make toffee shards, lightly grease large baking sheet with vegetable oil. Combine sugar and water in saucepan over low heat, stirring to dissolve sugar. Raise heat, bring to boil and cook, without stirring, until mixture turns golden, 7–8 minutes. Remove from heat and, using metal spoon, spoon mixture in patterns on baking sheet. Work quickly or toffee will set. Let toffee set 4–5 minutes, then break into pieces.

To serve, place oranges in individual bowls. Decorate with toffee shards.

Serves 6

Variation

Instead of making toffee shards, dip 8 whole figs into hot toffee in saucepan and place each coated fig on lightly greased baking sheet. Let stand until toffee is set. Serve 2 figs per person and top with heavy (whipping) cream.

WHISKEY ORANGES

Cantaloupe sorbet

1 cup (6¹/₂ oz/200 g) superfine (caster) sugar

1 cup (8 fl oz/250 ml) water

1 cantaloupe (rockmelon) (about 1¹/₂ lb/750 g),
   peeled, seeded and cut into chunks

2 tablespoons lime juice

Combine sugar and water in small saucepan over low heat and cook, stirring to dissolve sugar, about 3 minutes. Pour into a small container, cover and refrigerate until cold.

Place melon and lime juice in food processor and process until smooth. With motor running, gradually add chilled sugar syrup. Pour mixture into shallow metal pan and freeze, covered, until solid, 4–5 hours or overnight.

Break sorbet into pieces and place in food processor. Process until smooth and creamy, about 30 seconds. Return to metal pan, cover and freeze until just firm, about 30 minutes.

Scoop into individual dishes to serve.

Serves 4

CANTALOUPE SORBET

Raspberry and ricotta semifreddo

1 cup (8 oz/250 g) raspberries

1/2 cup (33/4 oz/110 g) superfine (caster) sugar, or more to taste

6 1/2 oz (200 g) ricotta

1 cup (8 fl oz/250 ml) heavy (double) cream

Place raspberries and sugar in food processor and process until smooth and sugar dissolves. Add more sugar if raspberries are tart. Add ricotta and cream and process until combined. Pour into freezerproof bowl, cover and freeze until firm, 4–5 hours or overnight.
Scoop in to individual dishes to serve.

Serves 4

Variation

Other seasonal berries, such as strawberries, blueberries or blackberries, in same quantity, can be used. Adjust sugar to taste. Two mangoes can also be substituted for raspberries.

RASPBERRY AND RICOTTA SEMIFREDDO

Watermelon and lime granita

1/2 cup (3³/4 oz/110 g) superfine (caster) sugar

1/2 cup (4 fl oz/125 ml) water

1/3 cup (3 fl oz/90 ml) lime juice

7 cups (3 lb/1.5 kg) seedless cubed watermelon

8 lime slices, for garnish

Combine sugar and water in small saucepan over low heat, stirring to dissolve sugar. Raise heat, bring to boil and cook until mixture is syrupy, 3–4 minutes. Remove from heat and stir in lime juice. Allow to cool.

Place watermelon, in batches, in food processor and process until smooth. Transfer to bowl and stir in lime syrup. Pour into shallow metal pan and freeze 3–4 hours, separating mixture with fork every 30 minutes, until mixture is consistency of shaved ice.

Serve in chilled bowls garnished with lime slices.

Serves 8

Pink grapefruit granita

2 cups (16 fl oz/500 ml) pink grapefruit juice

2 cups (16 fl oz/500 ml) orange juice

2 tablespoons vodka (optional)

1/3 cup (2 oz/60 g) caster sugar

Combine all ingredients in saucepan over low heat and cook, stirring to dissolve sugar, 2 minutes. Allow to cool. Pour into shallow metal pan and freeze 3–4 hours, separating mixture with fork every 30 minutes, until mixture is consistency of shaved ice.

Serve in chilled bowls.

Serves 6–8

WATERMELON AND LIME GRANITA

Rich chocolate and dried fruit cake

$^{3}/_{4}$ cup (4 oz/125 g) chopped candied (crystallized)
    apricots

$^{3}/_{4}$ cup (4 oz/125 g) chopped candied (crystallized) figs

$^{3}/_{4}$ cup (3 oz/90 g) chopped pitted prunes

$^{1}/_{3}$ cup (2 oz/60 g) chopped candied (crystallized)
    ginger

$^{1}/_{4}$ cup (2 fl oz/60 ml) brandy or dark rum

4 oz (125 g) unsalted butter

10 oz/300 g dark semisweet (plain) chocolate, chopped

2 eggs, separated

$^{1}/_{2}$ cup ($3^{3}/_{4}$ oz/110 g) superfine (caster) sugar

$^{1}/_{2}$ cup (4 oz/125 g) sour cream

1 cup (5 oz/150 g) all-purpose (plain) flour

1 teaspoon baking powder

$^{2}/_{3}$ cup ($2^{1}/_{2}$ oz/75 g) ground almonds

$^{1}/_{2}$ cup (2 oz/60 g) roughly chopped hazelnuts

FOR FROSTING

$6^{1}/_{2}$ oz (200 g) dark semisweet (plain) chocolate

$^{1}/_{2}$ cup (4 fl oz/125 ml) heavy (double) cream

Place fruit in large glass or ceramic bowl and stir in brandy or rum. Cover and let stand at room temperature 3–4 hours or overnight if possible, stirring occasionally. Preheat oven to 300°F (150°C/Gas 2). Grease 8-inch (20-cm) round cake pan with removable sides and line with parchment (baking paper).

Combine butter and chocolate in top part of double boiler or in metal bowl set over saucepan. Place over simmering water and allow mixture to melt, stirring to combine. Remove from heat and stir in egg yolks, sugar and sour cream. Sift together flour and baking powder into bowl. Fold into chocolate mixture alternating with almonds and hazelnuts. Beat egg whites in bowl using electric beaters until stiff peaks form. Fold into batter and pour into prepared pan. Bake until skewer inserted in middle of cake comes out clean. Let cool completely in pan before turning onto wire rack.

Meanwhile, to make frosting (icing), combine chocolate and cream in top part of double boiler or large metal bowl set over saucepan. Place over simmering water and allow to melt, stirring until combined. Allow to cool and whisk until frosting begins to thicken, about 1 minute.

Spread frosting over top of cake and serve.

Serves 10–12

RICH CHOCOLATE AND DRIED FRUIT CAKE

Dried fruit and lemon tea compote

2 cups (16 fl oz/500 ml) hot black tea

²/₃ cup (5 oz/150 g) packed brown
  sugar

¹/₄ cup (2 fl oz/60 ml) lemon juice

8 cardamom pods, gently crushed

¹/₄ lemon, thinly sliced

1 cup (6¹/₂ oz/200 g) dried pears

1 cup (3¹/₄ oz/100 g) dried apples

1 cup (6¹/₂ oz/200 g) dried figs,
  halved

FOR SPICED YOGURT

1¹/₂ cups (¹/₂ fl oz/375 ml) thick
  plain (natural) yogurt

¹/₄ cup (2 fl oz/60 ml) honey

¹/₂ teaspoon ground cinnamon

¹/₂ teaspoon ground cardamom

1 tablespoon finely grated orange zest

Combine hot tea, sugar, lemon juice and cardamom pods in bowl and stir to dissolve sugar. Place fruit in serving bowl and pour in hot lemon tea. Let stand at least three hours before serving.

Meanwhile, to make spiced yogurt, place all ingredients in bowl and stir to combine.

Serve compote in bowls. Top with spiced yogurt.

Serves 8

Dried-apricot jam

4 cups (1¹/₂ lb/750 g) dried apricots

8 cups (64 fl oz/2 L) water

¹/₄ cup (2 fl oz/60 ml) lemon juice

2 tablespoons finely grated lemon zest

4 cups (2 lb/1 kg) granulated sugar

A hint of lemon flavors this jam, which is an ideal breakfast accompaniment for toast, muffins and scones, as well as pancakes and waffles.

Place apricots in large glass or ceramic bowl and add water. Cover and let stand at room temperature for 24 hours.

Place apricots and water in large heavy saucepan and add lemon juice and zest. Bring to boil, reduce heat to medium-low and simmer, uncovered, until apricots are tender, about 30 minutes.

Add sugar, reduce heat to low and cook, stirring to dissolve sugar, 4–5 minutes. Raise heat, bring mixture to boil and cook, stirring occasionally, until jam sets when spoonful is placed on cold saucer, 20–25 minutes.

Pour into dry sterilized jars and seal immediately. Store in cool place for one week before using. Jam keeps for up to six months. Refrigerate after opening.

Makes about 3 cups (1¹/₂ lb/750 g)

DRIED FRUIT AND LEMON TEA COMPOTE

Raspberry jelly

4 cups (2 lb/1 kg) raspberries

2 cups (16 fl oz/500 ml) water

4 cups (2 lb/1 kg) granulated sugar,
  or as needed

Place raspberries and water in large heavy saucepan over low heat. Cook, uncovered, stirring occasionally, until raspberries are very soft, about 30 minutes. Line strainer with cheesecloth (muslin) and strain berries, without forcing them through cheesecloth, 3–4 hours. (Forcing them to extract juice will cloud jelly). There should be about 4 cups (32 fl oz/ 1 L) liquid.

For every cup of liquid, measure 1 cup (6$\frac{1}{2}$ oz/200 g) sugar and place in large baking pan over very low heat, stirring constantly, just until warm, about 5 minutes.

Bring raspberry liquid to boil and add warmed sugar. Adjust heat to maintain fast simmer and cook, uncovered, stirring occasionally, until jelly sets when spoonful is placed on cold plate, 15–20 minutes.

Pour into dry sterilized jars and seal immediately. Store in a cool place for one week before opening. Jelly keeps for up to six months. Refrigerate after opening.

Makes about 2 cups (1 lb/500 g)

Hints

Less sweet than many jellies, this raspberry jelly can be served for breakfast with toast or with roasted meats. It can also be heated and brushed over a fruit tart as a glaze.

RASPBERRY JELLY

Strawberry jam

4 cups (2 lb/1 kg) hulled (stemmed)
  strawberries

$^1/_3$ cup (3 fl oz/90 ml) lemon juice

4 cups (2 lb/1 kg) granulated sugar

Serve this luscious jam as an accompaniment to toast, brioches or scones, or use it to fill small pastry shells to serve with coffee.

Place strawberries and lemon juice in large heavy saucepan and bring to boil. Boil, uncovered, stirring occasionally, until strawberries are soft, 10 minutes. Place sugar in baking pan over very low heat, stirring constantly, just until warm, about 5 minutes. Add to strawberries, reduce heat to medium-low and cook, stirring occasionally, to dissolve sugar, 4–5 minutes. Adjust heat to maintain fast simmer and cook, uncovered, stirring occasionally until jam sets when spoonful is placed on cold plate, about 20 minutes.

Pour into dry sterilized jars and seal immediately. Store in cool place for two weeks before opening. Jam keeps for up to six months. Refrigerate after opening.

Quince jam

4 lb (2 kg) quinces, peeled,
  quartered, cored and thinly sliced

peels of 2 lemons, wrapped in a
  small cheesecloth (muslin) bag

$^1/_2$ cup (4 fl oz/125 ml) lemon juice

14 cups (112 fl oz/3.5 L) water

2 cups (1 lb/500 g) granulated sugar

This jam is delicious not only on hot buttered toast but also as an accompaniment to soft and semisoft cheeses. It can be spread on a leg of lamb, seasoned with fresh rosemary and garlic slivers, for roasting.

Place quince slices and lemon peels and juice in large heavy saucepan and add water. Simmer uncovered, stirring occasionally, until quinces are soft, about 1½ hours.

Remove muslin bag. Add sugar and stir over low heat to dissolve. Raise heat, bring to boil and boil rapidly, uncovered, stirring occasionally to prevent mixture from sticking, until jam sets when spoonful is placed on cold plate, 15–20 minutes.

Pour into dry sterilized jars and seal immediately. Store in cool place for four weeks before opening. Jam keeps for up to six months. Refrigerate after opening.

Makes about 8 cups (3 lb/1.5 kg)

STRAWBERRY JAM

Orange and lime marmalade

4 limes, halved and thinly sliced

2 oranges, halved and thinly sliced

10 cups (8 fl oz/2¹/₂ L) water

4 cups (2 lb/1 kg) sugar

Place lime and orange slices and water in large heavy saucepan, bring to boil, reduce heat and simmer, uncovered, for 1 hour.

Preheat oven to 250°F (130°C/Gas ¹/2). Place sugar in large baking pan and bake for 10 minutes, stirring after 5 minutes, until sugar is warm.

Bring fruit to boil and add sugar, stirring to dissolve. Adjust heat to maintain fast simmer and cook, uncovered, stirring occasionally, until jam sets when spoonful is placed on cold plate, about 30 minutes.

Pour into dry sterilized jars and seal immediately. Store in cool place for one week before opening. Jam keeps for up to six months. Refrigerate after opening.

Makes about 5 cups (30 oz/900 g)

Hints

Full of fruit, this marmalade is perfect served for breakfast for spreading on hot buttered brioche or toast. It can also be warmed and used to glaze fresh cream-filled cakes.

Mango chutney

6 or 7 mangoes (about 5 lb/2¹/₂ kg),
   peeled, pitted and sliced
2 Spanish (purple) onions, finely
   sliced
2 teaspoons black mustard seeds
2 teaspoons yellow mustard seeds
3 tablespoons finely chopped fresh
   ginger
3 cloves garlic, finely chopped
³/₄ cup (4 oz/125 g) dried currants
3 cups (1¹/₄ lb/625 g) packed brown
   sugar
2 cups (16 fl oz/500 ml) white wine
   vinegar

Make this chutney to serve with spicy Indian curries or with barbecued meat or fish. It is also an excellent spread on sandwiches filled with aged cheese and ham.

Combine all ingredients in large heavy saucepan over a low heat. Cook, stirring to dissolve sugar, about 5 minutes.
Raise heat and bring to boil. Reduce heat to medium and simmer, uncovered, stirring occasionally to prevent sticking, until mixture is thick, about 40 minutes.

Pour into dry sterilized jars and seal immediately. Store in cool dark place for one month before using. Chutney keeps for six months. Refrigerate after opening.

Makes about 6 cups (3 lb/1¹/2 kg)

Fresh pineapple pickle

¹/₂ cup (33/4 oz/110 g) packed brown
   sugar
¹/₂ cup (4 fl oz/125 ml) white wine
   vinegar
1 teaspoon yellow mustard seeds
1 teaspoon black mustard seeds
1 small pineapple (about 1¹/₂ lb/750
   g), peeled, cored and cut into 1-in
   (2.5-cm) chunks

Make this condiment for Christmas, to serve with holiday fare.

Combine sugar, vinegar and mustard seeds in large heavy saucepan over low heat. Cook, stirring to dissolve sugar, about 2 minutes.
Raise heat and bring to boil. Reduce heat to medium, add pineapple and simmer, uncovered, stirring occasionally, until liquid is syrupy and pineapple is translucent, about 15 minutes.

Pour into dry sterilized jars and seal immediately. Store in cool dark place for one week before using. Pickle keeps for one month. Refrigerate after opening.

Makes about 4 cups (2 lb/1 kg)

MANGO CHUTNEY

Preserved lemons

Spiced cherries

10 lemons

1 1/2 cups (8 oz/250 g) coarse sea salt

1/2 cup (4 fl oz/125 ml) lemon juice
plus 1/4 cup (2 fl oz/60 ml), or
more as needed

This traditional Moroccan preserve can be used to replace lemons in any savory recipe. It also makes a good tangy addition to salads, stuffings and casseroles.

Cut nine lemons in half and then each half into thirds. Slice remaining lemon.

Place salt in large glass or ceramic bowl and add lemon pieces, pressing salt into lemons and gently squeezing them to extract juice.

Pack lemons into sterilized jar, adding lemon slices at intervals for decoration. Spoon in any remaining salt and pour in remaining juice in bowl. Add extra juice if necessary so that lemons are completely covered.

Seal immediately and store in a cool dark place for at least two weeks before using. Preserved lemons keep for six months. Refrigerate after opening.

Makes 5–6 cups (40–48 fl oz/1 1/4–1 1/2 L)

8 cups (4 lb/2 kg) pitted, sweet dark cherries

2 1/2 cups (20 fl oz/600 ml) white wine vinegar

4 cups (2 lb/1 kg) granulated sugar

3 pieces fresh ginger (about 1 in/2 1/2 cm each), peeled

1 cinnamon stick

5 whole cloves

Spiced with ginger, cinnamon and cloves, these cherries can be served with Thanksgiving or Christmas turkey. As part of a cheese platter, they complement semisoft cheeses.

Place cherries in large glass or ceramic bowl. Select saucepan large enough to hold bowl and half fill with water. Place bowl in water and bring water to simmer. Cook, uncovered, until cherries are tender and start to release their juice, about 30 minutes.

Meanwhile, combine remaining ingredients in large saucepan over low heat and cook, stirring to dissolve sugar, 3–4 minutes. Raise heat and bring to boil. Reduce heat and simmer, uncovered, for 5 minutes. Remove ginger pieces,, cinnamon stick, and cloves.

Raise heat, bring liquid to boil and cook until thick, syrupy, and reduced by one-third, 5–7 minutes.

Spoon cherries and juice into dry sterilized jars, dividing evenly. Pour syrup over cherries and seal immediately. Store in cool place for at least one week before using. Cherries keep for up to six months. Refrigerate after opening.

Makes about 6 cups (3 lb/1 1/2 kg)

PRESERVED LEMONS

Cranberry marinade

1 1/2 cups (6 1/2 oz/200 g) cranberries

2 tablespoons red wine vinegar

1/4 cup (2 fl oz/60 ml) olive oil

2 tablespoons finely grated orange zest

2 cinnamon sticks

1 tablespoon finely grated fresh ginger

3 tablespoons packed brown sugar

Place cranberries in bowl and gently crush with back of fork. Add remaining ingredients and stir to combine and dissolve sugar.

Reserve 1/4 cup (2 fl oz/60 ml) marinade for basting if desired. Pour remaining marinade over poultry in glass or ceramic bowl and marinate, covered, in refrigerator, turning occasionally, for at least 3 hours or overnight. Baste meat regularly during cooking with reserved marinade.

Makes 2 cups (16 fl oz/500 ml)

Hints

This marinade is ideal for 2 lb (1 kg) poultry such as barbecued chicken thighs, broiled (grilled) turkey and duck breasts, roasted small whole chicken and chicken kebabs. A sauce can be made for roasted and broiled dishes by skimming the pan juices of as much fat as possible, placing the pan over medium heat and adding any remaining marinade. Boil sauce rapidly until reduced by half and slightly syrupy.

CRANBERRY MARINADE

Raspberry marinade

1 cup (8 oz/250 g) raspberries

1/4 cup (2 fl oz/60 ml) raspberry vinegar

1/2 cup (4 fl oz/125 ml) olive oil

1/4 cup (1/3 oz/10 g) fresh tarragon leaves

freshly ground pepper

Pair this marinade with panfried, roasted or broiled (grilled) chicken pieces or fish fillets. The quantity here is suitable for 1 1/2 lb (750 g) poultry or fish. Reserve some of the marinade for adding to pan juices to make a sauce. Cook the sauce over high heat, stirring, until reduced by half. Add 1 cup (8 fl oz/250 ml) chicken or fish stock to the reduced sauce and simmer until heated through, then serve.

Place raspberries in bowl and gently crush with back of fork so raspberries are still whole but some of juice is extracted. Stir in remaining ingredients and season with pepper. Reserve ¼ cup (2 fl oz/60 ml) marinade for basting, if desired. Pour remaining marinade over chicken or fish in glass or ceramic bowl and marinate covered, in refrigerator, turning occasionally, for at least 3 hours or overnight. Baste chicken or fish regularly during cooking with reserved marinade.

Makes 2½ cups (20 fl oz/625 ml)

Thai lime marinade

1 cup (8 fl oz/250 ml) coconut milk

1/4 cup (2 fl oz/60 ml) olive oil

1/4 cup (2 fl oz/60 ml) lime juice

2 tablespoons finely grated lime zest

1 tablespoon finely grated fresh ginger

2 cloves garlic, crushed

2 small red chili peppers, thinly sliced

2 tablespoons packed brown sugar

1 tablespoon fish sauce

The combination of lime juice and zest, coconut milk and ginger makes a perfect complement for seafood. This recipe is suitable for 2 lb (1 kg) shrimp (prawns), baby octopus or fish fillets.

Combine all ingredients in bowl and stir to combine and dissolve sugar. Let stand overnight, covered, in refrigerator before using, to allow flavors to combine.

Reserve 1/4 cup (2 fl oz/60 ml) marinade for basting, if desired. Pour remaining marinade over seafood in glass or ceramic bowl and marinate, covered, in refrigerator, turning occasionally, for at least 3 hours or overnight. Baste fish regularly during cooking with reserved marinade.

Makes 2 cups (16 fl oz/500 ml)

Red wine, cherry and thyme marinade

2 cups (1 lb/500 g) pitted, sweet dark cherries

1 cup (8 fl oz/250 ml) dry red wine

2 cloves garlic, crushed

3 or 4 sprigs thyme

Use this rich-hued and robust marinade for four beef steaks such as sirloin, T-bone or rump, each about 10 oz (300 g). Either panfry the steaks or cook them in a ridged grill pan.

Place cherries in bowl and gently crush with back of fork so cherries are still whole but some of juice is extracted. Stir in remaining ingredients.

Reserve ¼ cup (2 fl oz/60 ml) marinade for basting, if desired. Pour remaining marinade over beef in glass or ceramic bowl and marinate covered in refrigerator overnight, turning once. When cooking beef, season with salt and pepper, and baste regularly with reserved marinade. Add cherries to pan for last 2–3 minutes of cooking. Serve cherries and pan juices as sauce on side.

Makes 3 cups (24 fl oz/750 ml)

Sweet-and-spicy sour pineapple marinade

1 small pineapple (about 1½ lb/750 g), peeled, cut lengthwise into quarters, cored and thinly sliced

½ cup (4 fl oz/125 ml) pineapple juice

¼ cup (2 fl oz/60 ml) lime juice

2 cloves garlic, crushed

1 small red chili pepper, finely chopped

¼ cup (2 oz/60 g) packed brown sugar

Sweet from the fruit and spicy from the chilli pepper, this recipe pairs well with pork, such as spareribs or chops, that are barbecued or cooked in a ridged grill pan. It is also a good for kebobs made with pieces of pork fillet threaded onto wooden skewers. The remaining marinade can be boiled for 4–5 minutes, until mixture is reduced and pineapple is translucent, and served as a sauce for the cooked meat.

Combine all ingredients in bowl. Reserve ¼ cup (2 fl oz/60 ml) marinade for basting, if desired. Pour remaining marinade over meat in glass or ceramic bowl and marinate, covered, in refrigerator overnight, turning occasionally. Baste meat regularly during cooking with reserved marinade.

Makes 4–5 cups (32–40 fl oz/1–1¼ L)

Grapefruit and honey marinade

$^1/_2$ cup (4 fl oz/125 ml) grapefruit juice

1 grapefruit, peeled, pith removed, cut into
   segments and seeded

$^1/_4$ cup (3 oz/90 g) honey

$^1/_4$ cup (2 fl oz/60 ml) brandy

$^1/_4$ cup (2 fl oz/60 ml) dry white wine

2 tablespoons fresh thyme leaves

freshly ground pepper

Combine all ingredients in bowl. Reserve ¼ cup (2 fl oz/60 ml) marinade for basting, if desired. Pour remaining marinade over meat in glass or ceramic bowl and marinate, covered, in refrigerator, turning occasionally, for at least 3 hours or overnight. Baste meat regularly during cooking with reserved marinade.

Makes 4 cups (32 fl oz/1 L)

Hints

Cuts of lamb, including a whole leg, for broiling (grilling), roasting or barbecuing, are especially good flavored with this marinade. Serve broiled or roasted meat with the skimmed pan juices as a sauce. This quantity is suitable for up to 2¼ lb (1.1 kg) meat.

GRAPEFRUIT AND HONEY MARINADE

Pineapple-lime cooler

3 cups (24 fl oz/750 ml) pineapple juice

2 tablespoons lime juice

2 tablespoons superfine (caster) sugar, or more as
needed

12 ice cubes

1 cup (8 fl oz/250 ml) club soda (soda water)

4 lime slices (optional)

Place pineapple juice, lime juice, sugar and ice cubes in food processor or blender and process until ice is crushed and mixture is smooth. Taste for sugar and add more, 1 teaspoon at a time, if cooler is tart.

To serve, pour into tall glasses until two-thirds full, top with club soda and serve immediately, garnished with lime slices if desired.

Serves 4

PINEAPPLE·LIME COOLER

Iced lemon tea

5 teaspoons black tea

6 cups (48 fl oz/1.5 L) boiling water

1/4 cup (2 fl oz/60 ml) lemon juice

1/4 cup (13/4 oz/50 g) superfine
  (caster) sugar

1 lemon, sliced

2 sprigs lemon thyme

ice cubes

Place tea in large teapot and add boiling water. Let stand 5 minutes to infuse.

Strain into heatproof container and add lemon juice and sugar, stirring to dissolve sugar. Add lemon slices and thyme and chill, covered, in refrigerator, for at least 1 hour. To serve, place ice cubes in glasses and pour in chilled tea.

Serves 4

Lemon-limeade

1/2 cup (4 fl oz/125 ml) lemon juice

1/2 cup (4 fl oz/125 ml) lime juice

1 cup (61/2 oz/200 g) superfine
  (caster) sugar

4 cups (32 fl oz/1 L) club soda (soda
  water)

8–10 mint leaves

ice cubes

Combine lemon juice, lime juice and sugar in small saucepan over low heat and cook, stirring to dissolve sugar, 3–4 minutes. Remove from heat and pour into heatproof container. Refrigerate, covered, until completely cold, about 2 hours.

To serve, add club soda and mint leaves and stir to combine. Place ice cubes in glasses and pour in lemon-limeade. Light rum, vodka or tequila can be added to make alcoholic drink.

Serves 4

Healthy yogurt-fruit drink

4 cups (32 fl oz/1 L) soy milk

1 cup (8 fl oz/250 ml) plain
  (natural) yogurt

2 tablespoons honey, or more as
  needed

Choice of fruit: 4 kiwifruit (Chinese
  gooseberries), peeled and halved;
  1 cup (8 oz/250 g) hulled (stemmed)
  strawberries; 2 bananas, peeled
  and sliced; 1 cup (8 oz/250 g)
  raspberries; 2 mangoes
  (about 11/2 lb/750 g), peeled,
  pitted and cut into chunks

Combine all ingredients in food processor or blender and add fruit of choice. Process until smooth. Add more honey if desired.

Serve immediately or refrigerate until ready to serve.

Serves 4

Low-fat banana smoothie

4 cups (32 fl oz/1 L) nonfat milk

1 cup (8 fl oz/250 ml) low-fat plain
  (natural) yogurt

2 bananas, peeled and sliced

Combine all ingredients in food processor or blender and process until smooth.

Serve immediately or refrigerate until ready to serve.

Serves 4

HEALTHY YOGURT-FRUIT DRINK

Index

Apples
 baked 66
 and date cake 32
 pie 34
Apricots
 dried apricot jam 86
 Moroccan lamb tagine with 20
 pear and cherry crumble, brandied 70

Baked apples 66
Bananas
 healthy yogurt-fruit drink 106
 smoothie, low-fat 106
 tropical fruit salad with lime syrup 30
 warm cake, with caramel bananas 48
Bavarian cream with plums 56
Beef fillet braised with quinces 14
Bell pepper, red, and mango salad 30
Berry bread-and-butter puddings 62
Blackberry sauce 58
Black currant syrup, pears in 52
Blueberry
 and almond mini muffins 36
 cheesecakes 36
Brandied pear, cherry and apricot crumble 70
Bread-and-butter berry puddings 62
Butternut squash and green papaya salad 28

Cake
 apple and date 32
 kiwifruit sponge 38
 old-fashioned lemon 42
 orange, with plum glaze 42
 warm banana, with caramel bananas 48
Cantaloupe sorbet 78
Capsicum (bell pepper), red, and mango salad 30
Cheesecakes, blueberry 36

Cherries
 pear and apricot crumble, brandied 70
 and red currants, lamb cutlets with 18
 red wine and thyme marinade 101
 spiced 96
 trifle 64
Chicken
 roast, with pickled kumquats
  and polenta 12
 stuffed with prunes 10
Chinese gooseberries see Kiwifruit
Chocolate
 and dried fruit cake, rich 84
  pear tartlets 44
Chutney, mango 94
Citrus pickled shrimp, spicy 24
Cooler, pineapple-lime 104
Cranberry marinade 98
Crumble, brandied pear, cherry and apricot 70
Currants
 black, syrup, pears in 52
 red, and cherries, lamb cutlets with 18
Custard, vanilla, peaches with 54

Dark cherry trifle 64
Date and apple cake 32
Dried-apricot jam 86
Dried fruit
 and chocolate cake, rich 84
 and lemon tea compote 86

Escallops of pork with purple grapes 22

Fresh pineapple pickle 94
Fruit salad, tropical, with lime syrup 30

Gingerbread, upside-down pear 46
Gingered litchi sauce 60
Granita
 pink grapefruit 82
 watermelon and lime 82

Grapefruit
    and honey marinade 102
    pink, granita 82
Grapes, purple, escallops of pork with 22
Green papaya and butternut squash salad 28

Healthy yogurt-fruit drink 106

Iced lemon tea 106

Jam
    dried-apricot 86
    quince 90
    strawberry 90
Jelly, raspberry 88

Kiwifruit
    cucumber, orange and cashew salad 28
    healthy yogurt-fruit drink 106
    sponge cake 38
Kumquats, pickled, with roast chicken and polenta 12

Lamb
    cutlets with red currant and cherries 18
    tagine, Moroccan, with apricots 20
Lemons
    cake, old-fashioned 42
    and dried fruit tea compote 86
    iced tea 106
    limeade 106
    and oranges, osso bucco with 16
    preserved 96
    spicy citrus-pickled shrimp 24
    tart 40
Lime
    lemonade 106
    marinade, Thai 100
    and orange marmalade 92
    pineapple cooler 104
    spicy citrus-pickled shrimp 24
    and watermelon granita 82
Litchi sauce, gingered 60
Low-fat banana smoothie 106
Lychee (litchi) sauce, gingered 60

Mango
    chutney 94
    healthy yogurt-fruit drink 106
    and passionfruit slice 60
    and red bell pepper salsa 30
    salad and basil oil, salmon fillets with 26
    and strawberries with zabaglione 72
    tropical fruit salad with lime syrup 30
Marinade
    cranberry 98
    grapefruit and honey 102
    raspberry 100
    red wine, cherry and thyme 101
    Thai lime 100
Marmalade, orange and lime 92
Melon see Cantaloupe; Watermelon
Moroccan lamb tagine with apricots 20
Muffins, blueberry and almond 36

Old-fashioned lemon cake 42
Oranges
    cake with plum glaze 42
    kiwifuit, cucumber and cashew salad 28
    and lemons, osso bucco with 16
    and lime marmalade 92
    whiskey 76
Osso busso with oranges and lemons 16

Panfried pineapple 68
Papaya
    green, and butternut squash salad 28
    tropical fruit salad with lime syrup 30
Passion fruit
    and mango slice 60
    tropical fruit salad with lime syrup 30
Peaches with vanilla custard 54
Pears
    in black currant syrup 52
    cherry and apricot crumble, brandied 70
    chocolate tartlets 44
    gingerbread, upside down 46
Pickle, fresh pineapple 94
Pie, apple 34

Pineapple
    lime cooler 104
    marinade, sweet-and-spicy sour 101
    panfried 68
    pickle 94
    tropical fruit salad with lime syrup 30
Pink grapefruit granita 82
Plums
    with Bavarian cream 56
    glaze, orange cake with 42
Pork, escallops of, with purple grapes 22
Preserved lemons 96
Prunes, chicken stuffed with 10
Puddings, bread-and-butter berry 62

Quinces
    beef fillet braised with 14
    jam 90

Raspberry
    cream, strawberries in 72
    healthy yogurt-fruit drink 106
    jelly 88
    marinade 100
    and ricotta semifreddo 80
Red bell pepper and mango salad 30
Red currants and cherries, lamb cutlets with 18
Red wine, cherry and thyme marinade 101
Rich chocolate and druit fruit cake 84
Roast chicken with pickled kumquats and polenta 12
Rockmelon (cantaloup) sorbet 78

Salad
    green papaya and butternut squash 28
    kiwifuit, cucumber, orange and cashew salad 28
    mango, and basil oil, salmon fillets with 26
    mango and red bell pepper 30
    tropical fruit, with lime syrup 30
Salmon fillets with mango salad and basil oil 26
Sauce
    blackberry 58
    gingered litchi 60

Semifreddo, raspberry and ricotta 80
Shortcakes, strawberry 50
Shrimp, spicy citrus-pickled 24
Slice, mango and passionfruit 60
Smoothie, low-fat banana 106
Sorbet, cantaloupe 78
Spiced cherries 96
Spicy citrus-pickled shrimp 24
Sponge cake, kiwifruit 38
Squash, butternut, and green papaya
        salad 28
Strawberries
    healthy yogurt-fruit drink 106
    jam 90
    and mangoes with zabaglione 72
    in raspberry cream 72
    shortcakes 50
Sweet-and-spicy sour pineapple marinade 101

Tart, lemon 40
Tartlets, chocolate pear 44
Tea, iced lemon 106
Thai lime marinade 100
Trifle, dark cherry 64
Tropical fruit salad with lime syrup 30

Upside-down pear gingerbread 46

Veal osso busso with oranges and lemons 16

Warm banana cake with caramel
        bananas 48
Watermelon
    gelatin 74
    and lime granita 82
Whiskey oranges 76

Yogurt-fruit drink 106

Zabaglione with strawberries and mangoes 72

Guide to weights and measures

The conversions given in the recipes in this book are approximate. Whichever system you choose, the important thing to remember is to ensure the balance remains the same thoughout the ingredients. If you follow all the metric measures you will end up with the same proportions as if you followed all the imperial.

DRY MEASURES

Imperial	Metric
$1/6$ oz	5 g
$1/2$ oz	15 g
1 oz	30 g
2 oz	60 g
3 oz	90 g
$3^1/2$ oz	100 g
4 oz ($1/4$ lb)	125 g
5 oz	150 g
6 oz	180 g
$6^1/2$ oz	200 g
7 oz	220 g
8 oz ($1/2$ lb)	250 g
9 oz	280 g
10 oz	300 g
11 oz	330 g
12 oz ($3/4$ lb)	375 g
13 oz	400 g
14 oz	440 g
15 oz	470 g
16 oz (1 lb)	500 g
24 oz ($1^1/2$ lb)	750 g
32 oz (2 lb)	1 kg
3 lb	1.5 kg
4 lb	2 kg

LIQUID MEASURES

Imperial	Metric	Cup
1 fl oz	30 ml	
2 fl oz	60 ml	$1/4$ cup
3 fl oz	90 ml	$1/3$ cup
4 fl oz	125 ml	$1/2$ cup
5 fl oz	150 ml	$2/3$ cup
6 fl oz	180 ml	$3/4$ cup
8 fl oz	250 ml	1 cup
10 fl oz	300 ml	$1^1/2$ cups
14 oz	450 ml	2 cups
16 fl oz	500 ml	2 cups
24 fl oz	750 ml	3 cups
32 fl oz	1000 ml (1 litre)	4 cups

USEFUL CONVERSIONS

$1/4$ teaspoon	1.25 ml
$1/2$ teaspoon	2.5 ml
1 teaspoon	5 ml
1 Australian tablespoon	20 ml (4 teaspoons)
1 UK/US tablespoon	15 ml (3 teaspoons)

Butter/Shortening

1 tablespoon	$1/2$ oz	15 g
$1^1/2$ tablespoons	$3/4$ oz	20 g
2 tablespoons	1 oz	30 g
3 tablespoons	$1^1/2$ oz	50 g

Sifted all-purpose (plain) flour/dried breadcrumbs/chopped nuts/grated cheddar

2 tablespons	$1/2$ oz	15 g
$1/4$ cup	1 oz	30 g
$1/3$ cup	$1^1/2$ oz	50 g
$1/2$ cup	2 oz	60 g
$2/3$ cup	3 oz	90 g
1 cup	4 oz	125 g

OVEN TEMPERATURE GUIDE

The Celcius ($^\circ$C) and Fahrenheit ($^\circ$F) temperatures in this chart relate to most electric ovens. Decrease by 25°F or 10°C for gas ovens or refer to the manufacturer's temperature guide. For temperatures below 325°F (160°C) do not decrease the given temperature.

Oven description	$^\circ$C	$^\circ$F	Gas Mark
Cool	100	200	$1/4$
Very slow	120	250	$1/2$
Slow	150	300	2
Warm	160	325	3
Moderate	180	350	4
Moderately hot	190	375	5
Moderately hot	200	400	6
Hot	220	425	7
Very hot	230	450	8
Extremely hot	250	500	10

First published in the United States in 1999 by Periplus Editions (HK) Ltd., with editorial offices at
153 Milk Street, Boston, Massachusetts 02109 and 5 Little Road #08-01 Singapore 536983

Library of Congress Catalog Card Number: 99-60842

ISBN: 962 593 461 8

DISTRIBUTED BY

USA
Tuttle Publishing
Distribution Center
Airport Industrial Park
364 Innovation Drive
North Clarendon, VT 05759-9436
Tel: (802) 773 8930
Tel: (800) 526 2778

Japan
Tuttle Publishing
RK Building, 2nd Floor
2-13-10 Shimo-Meguro, Meguro-Ku
Tokyo 153 0064
Tel: (03) 5437 0171
Fax: (03) 5437 0755

Canada
Raincoast Books
9050 Shaughnessy Street
Vancouver
British Columbia
V6P 6E5
Tel: (604) 323 7100
Fax: (604) 323 2600

Southeast Asia
Berkeley Books Pte. Ltd.
5 Little Road #08-01
Singapore 536983
Tel: (65) 280-1330
Fax: (65) 280-6290

First Edition
05 04 03 02 01 00   10 9 8 7 6 5 4 3 2

Printed in Singapore